Contents

*Words in bold, **like this**, are in the Glossary.*

1 The units of life

A cell is a remarkable thing. It is a tiny package of chemicals, too small to be seen without the help of a microscope. Each of these packages has all the properties of life. Some living things, such as **bacteria**, are single cells, but the plants and animals we see around us, and ourselves as well, are made up of great assemblies of cells, millions upon millions of them.

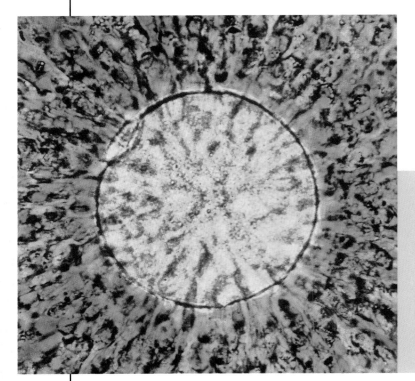

In this book we will be concentrating on the different groups of cells that make up animals, and how they work together. But before we start, we need to learn a little more about what cells are.

Animals and plants are made up of millions upon millions of cells. Even the biggest organism starts off as just a single cell, like the human egg cell shown here (yellow). The blue cells around the egg support and nourish it while it is growing. This is a false-colour photo. Magnification approx. x 560.

Cell types

There are two different types of cell. The simplest cells are the bacteria, which are called **prokaryote** cells. Prokaryote cells have a very simple structure. Around the outside is a thin **membrane**, usually surrounded by a thicker, rigid cell wall. Inside the membrane is a jelly-like mixture of substances, in which all the processes that allow the bacterium to grow and reproduce happen. The genetic material (that holds all the information to make a new bacterium) is contained in this mixture, called the **cytoplasm**.

The other basic cell type incorporates all other cells, including all the cells that make up plants and animals. These cells are bigger than those of bacteria. Even before electron microscopes became available in the 1960s, biologists had realized that, unlike prokaryotes, these bigger cells had many different structures inside them.

These more complex cells are called **eukaryotes**. Eukaryote cells are divided up inside into compartments called **organelles**, each one surrounded by its own membrane. One of these compartments is the **nucleus**, which contains the cell's genetic material. The word eukaryote means 'true nucleus' and the word prokaryote means 'before the nucleus'.

Becoming multicellular

In the simplest living things, a single cell carries out all the different functions of life, for instance feeding, moving, dividing, and getting rid of waste. More complex living things have many millions of cells, and not all of them are the same. Different types of cells develop and each is specialized to carry out a particular task. The nerve cells of an animal, for instance, are specialized to transmit electrical impulses from one cell to another. Some cells supply food, some transport food and wastes, some transmit information or instructions, some provide support and others have the job of reproducing (producing **offspring**).

The many different types of cell in an animal or plant work closely together. Being multicellular means that cells must cooperate on a vast scale. This cooperation must work perfectly, time after time after time. All around us, in every plant or animal in the living world, we can see the results of this incredible interaction between millions upon millions of living cells.

Sponges (pink) among sea anemones (orange). Sponges are some of the simplest multicellular animals. They do not have the specialized types of cells, such as nerves and muscles, that are found in more complex animals.

Animal cells

A typical animal cell and a typical plant cell have many similarities, but there are some important differences. In this section we will look at animal cells and what makes them different from plant cells.

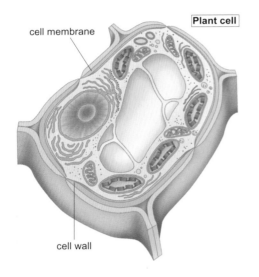

Plant cell

cell membrane

cell wall

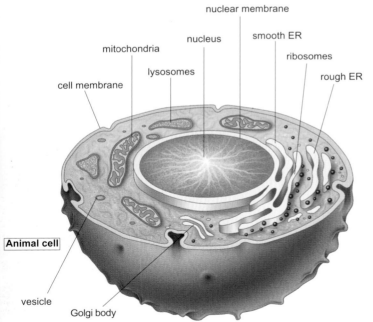

nuclear membrane

mitochondria

nucleus

smooth ER

lysosomes

ribosomes

cell membrane

rough ER

Animal cell

vesicle

Golgi body

Unlike plants, animal cells do not have a cell wall. This illustration shows other typical features of an animal cell.

Both animal and plant cells are surrounded by a thin cell **membrane**. This is the boundary of the cell, separating it from the external environment. The membrane holds the cell together and controls what passes in and out. It lets some things in but not others, and for this reason it is described as a partially permeable membrane.

Animal cells are smaller than plant cells – the average animal cell is about half the size of a plant cell. This makes them more difficult to see under the microscope, but the main reason that plant cells are easier to see is that they are surrounded by a thick, rigid cell wall. One of the main features of animal cells is that they do not have a surrounding wall. This gives an animal cell much more flexibility than a plant cell. Most animals are mobile creatures – they move about – so this flexibility is very important.

Cell control centre

Within both animal and plant cells there is a large **nucleus**. This is the cell's control centre. It guides the activities of the cell by providing the instructions for building **proteins**. Proteins manage the day-to-day running of cells. Special proteins called **enzymes** control chemical activity by regulating the speeds of the many chemical reactions within the cell. Without enzymes, the reactions would virtually grind to a halt and life would cease.

Between the nucleus and the cell membrane is the **cytoplasm**. This is where the ceaseless chemical activities of the cell take place. Here the cell obtains energy from its food, carries out repairs and makes new cell components. Hundreds of chemical reactions go on constantly, guided by the enzymes made according to instructions from the nucleus. Together, these reactions make up the cell's **metabolism**.

Animal cell objectives

The billions of cells within an animal work together to provide the greatest benefit for all. Whatever the animal might be, whether a human, a kangaroo, an albatross or a starfish, the cells are organized to perform four vital tasks:

1 To keep the conditions within the animal's body at the best levels for cells to work efficiently.
2 To get **nutrients** from food, and to carry the nutrients to all cells of the body, disposing of cell wastes.
3 To defend the animal against disease-causing micro-organisms.
4 To reproduce – and to get the next generation off to a good start.

We will see in later sections of the book how animal cells carry out these four vital tasks.

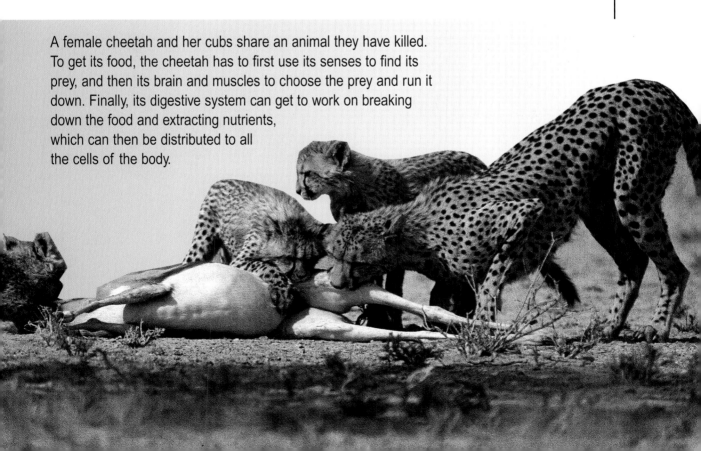

A female cheetah and her cubs share an animal they have killed. To get its food, the cheetah has to first use its senses to find its prey, and then its brain and muscles to choose the prey and run it down. Finally, its digestive system can get to work on breaking down the food and extracting nutrients, which can then be distributed to all the cells of the body.

Working together

A single-celled organism has to carry out all the functions necessary for its survival. In a multicellular animal, jobs such as getting food, removing waste and moving **nutrients** around the body are divided up between groups of cells that have become specialized to perform these particular tasks.

Tissues

Groups of similar cells that work together to perform a particular job in an organism are called **tissues**. For example, muscle tissue is made up of cells that can shorten (contract) to make the animal move. Animal tissues can be classified into just four main types:
- epithelial tissue
- connective tissue
- muscle
- nervous tissue.

Epithelial tissue

Epithelial tissue is commonly referred to as **epithelium**. Epithelial tissues either form an outer skin (for example, human skin and hair, or the scales of a snake), or an inner lining (for example, inside a blood vessel). Epithelial cells are packed closely together to form an unbroken layer.

Stratified epithelium has two or more layers of cells and gives protection. The outer layer of your skin is a good example of stratified epithelium.

Simple or squamous epithelium is a single layer of cells that acts as a lining. It covers many surfaces in the body, including the lining of blood vessels and the walls of the tiny air sacs (**alveoli**) that make up the lungs. The cells that make up squamous epithelium are very thin and smooth and flat. They fit tightly together, to form a smooth surface over which fluids can flow easily.

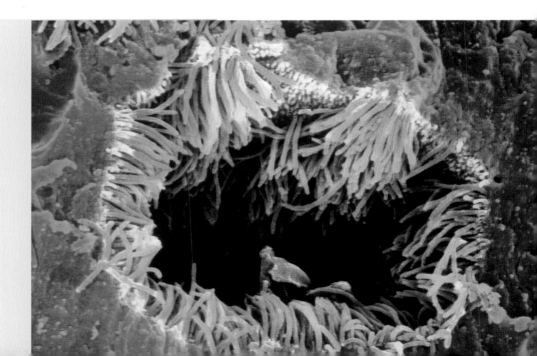

A false-colour photo taken with a scanning electron microscope showing the ciliated epithelium lining the bronchioles (tubes) in the lungs. The cilia are coloured green. Magnification approx. x 3600.

Ciliated epithelium is made up of cells covered with **cilia** – tiny, hair-like projections from the surface of the cell. Cilia move backwards and forwards with a regular beat, rather like oars. Some single-celled creatures have cilia, which move them around. In ciliated epithelium the cells stay in one place, and the 'rowing' of the cilia moves fluids on the surface of the epithelium. For example, the **bronchioles** (tubes) of the lungs are lined with cilia, and the lining is covered with a layer of **mucus**. This mucus traps dirt and other particles. The movement of the cilia moves the dirty mucus up and out of the lungs.

Connective tissue

There are more types of connective tissue than any other types of tissue. Some connective tissues are soft – they surround and connect together other tissues and organs. Other connective tissues are hard and have the job of supporting and protecting the body (bone and cartilage are examples of this kind of tissue). Blood, which consists of a mixture of cells and a fluid called **plasma**, is also classified as a connective tissue.

Muscle

Muscle is made up of cells that have the ability to shorten (contract). Muscle cells are long and can contract to between a half and a third of their length. Muscle tissue is used for movement. Muscle contractions are responsible for the beating of the heart, which moves blood around the body. Other muscles squeeze food along the tubes of the digestive system. Also, the contractions of muscles connected to an animal's skeleton move its body around.

Nervous tissue

Nervous tissue is made up of highly specialized cells that transmit electrical signals, called nerve impulses, throughout the body. These nerve impulses move quickly through the body, for example carrying information about the outside world from the eyes or other senses, or carrying impulses from the brain to the muscles.

Tendons are tissues that connect muscles to bones – they are a type of connective tissue. Tendons are made mostly of a fibrous protein called collagen. Bundles of collagen fibres are shown here. Magnification approx. x 70.

Organs and organ systems

The four tissue types that make up complex animals are not scattered randomly through their bodies. Groups of tissues are arranged together to form the organs, and in more complex animals these organs work together in organ systems.

Organs

The heart, the lungs, the brain and the stomach are all examples of organs. Each organ is specialized to do a job, or a range of jobs, and no other organ can take on that job. The lungs, for example, are specialized to take in oxygen from the air, and get rid of carbon dioxide. If the lungs are damaged and cannot work, the heart cannot take over this job; nor can the stomach, or the brain.

An organ is usually made up of several types of tissue. The human heart, for example, is made up of muscle tissue, nerve tissue and connective tissue, while the stomach is formed from **epithelial** tissue, gland tissue and muscle tissue.

Systems

An organ system is made up of two or more organs working together to perform some task that is of benefit to the whole organism. Major organ systems include the circulatory system (in humans this is the heart and blood vessels), which is the body's main transport system; the digestive system, which breaks down food into useful **nutrients** that the animal can use; and the reproductive system, which is responsible for producing **offspring**.

The survival of an animal depends on all its organ systems working together. Each one is just as important as the others. Think of a car. If the electrical system fails it won't go anywhere, even if it has four new tyres and a full tank of fuel.

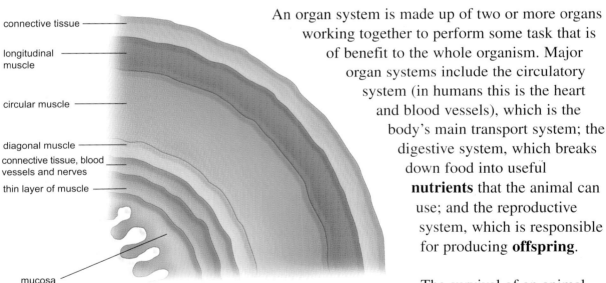

connective tissue

longitudinal muscle

circular muscle

diagonal muscle

connective tissue, blood vessels and nerves

thin layer of muscle

mucosa (epithelium with digestive glands)

The stomach is made up of different tissues, including epithelial and gland tissue, as well as several layers of muscle tissue, as this illustration shows.

A bat catching insects. To catch food, many different organ systems must work together. For instance, the bat flight muscles are directed by the nervous system, and they get the energy they need to move using nutrients from the digestive system and oxygen supplied by the circulatory system.

An animal is much the same. The blood vessels that are part of the circulatory system take nutrients and oxygen to the cells of the body, and take away their wastes. However, the nutrients in the blood come from the digestive system (which breaks down food to release the nutrients), and oxygen gets into the blood via the lungs (which are part of the respiratory, or gas exchange, system). All three of these systems use the nervous system to pass messages from one area to another and to get information from the senses and instructions from the brain. If your nervous system failed, you wouldn't be able to coordinate your movements to find food, and you wouldn't be able to see or feel the food even if you found it.

The organized organism

A multicelled organism is the total of all its cells, tissues, organs and organ systems all intimately linked together. No single system could sustain life without the others. No system can go on working if a major organ fails – imagine the circulatory system without the heart, or the nervous system without the brain. No organ can continue to function if all its tissues are damaged.

The hundred million million cells that make up your body are all working together to ensure their survival – and yours!

2 On the outside

The bodies of human beings and many other animals are covered by an outer protective layer – the skin. However, the skin of each type of animal is different. Mammals have skin that is covered by hair. Those that live in cold climates tend to have long, thick hair that keeps them warm, while those living in hotter areas have shorter, thinner hair. The hair may be coloured and patterned to provide camouflage. Instead of hair, the skin of a bird is covered with feathers, while fishes and reptiles have a layer of thin, flexible overlapping scales. The skin of frogs, toads and other amphibians does not have any covering at all.

In human beings, the skin is almost completely waterproof. This prevents the escape of blood and other fluids from the body. The skin also acts as a barrier to prevent disease-causing **bacteria** and other harmful things from getting into the body.

Skin structure

Your skin is actually an organ – in fact it is the largest organ in your body. As well as the layers of skin cells, it includes hair, nails and glands. The skin has three layers: the epidermis, the dermis and the subcutaneous tissue.

The epidermis is the outermost layer of the skin. It is about as thick as a sheet of paper over most parts of the body. The epidermis is made up of several layers of cells. The outermost layer consists of dying cells filled with a waterproof **protein** called keratin. The keratin is what gives skin its toughness. The innermost layer is mainly a single row of tall, narrow cells. These continually divide to replace the cells that are constantly being lost from the outer surface. Also in the innermost layer are cells called melanocytes. These produce a brownish black pigment called melanin, which gives skin its colour.

This cross-section through human skin shows the epidermis, the dermis and the outermost portion of subcutaneous tissue.

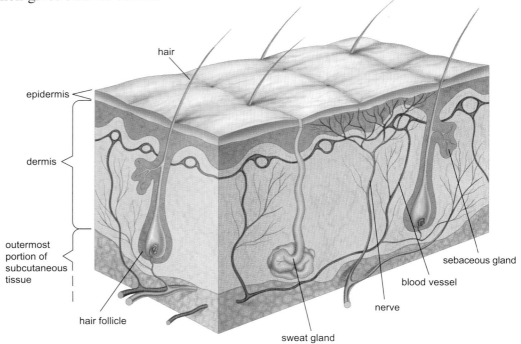

hair

epidermis

dermis

outermost portion of subcutaneous tissue

hair follicle

sweat gland

nerve

blood vessel

sebaceous gland

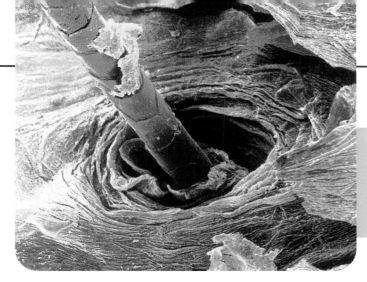

Photo of a human hair projecting from the skin, taken with a scanning electron microscope. Magnification approx. x 340.

The middle layer of the skin, the dermis, is between 15 and 40 times thicker than the epidermis. It is made up of a network of blood vessels, nerve endings and connective tissue. On the surface of the dermis there are many tiny projections that contain nerve endings that are sensitive to touch. These fit into pits in the innermost layer of the epidermis and are found in greatest numbers on the palms and fingertips. The innermost layer of the skin is called subcutaneous tissue. It varies greatly in thickness, but is much thicker than both the epidermis and dermis. It is made up of blood vessels, connective tissue, and fat-storing cells. The subcutaneous tissue helps to prevent heat loss from the body and to cushion blows.

Hair, nails and glands

Most of the skin, with the exception of the soles of the feet and the palms of the hands, is covered with hairs. The only living part of a hair is the bulb, at the root of the hair. The bulb is found beneath the surface of the skin in the dermis, enclosed in a structure called a follicle. The hair cells contain a hard form of keratin.

A nail has three parts: the plate (the hard outer part), the bed (the part beneath the plate) and the matrix (this lies under the surface of the skin at the base of the nail). Both the bed and the plate cells are formed in the matrix. Older cells are pushed towards the tip of the nail by new cells growing at the base. These older cells contain keratin.

The skin has two kinds of glands, sebaceous glands and sweat glands. Sebaceous glands secrete an oil called sebum into the hair follicles. This lubricates the hair and the surface of the skin. Sweat glands produce the sweat, a salty fluid, that cools the body as it evaporates. They are found all over the skin. Some are working continually, but others only release sweat when the body is overheating because it is working hard, or because the outside temperature is high. Sweating is one of the mechanisms the body uses to keep its internal temperature at the optimum level for cell activity.

3 Movement and support

All but the very simplest animals have some type of muscle. The muscles of human beings and those of other animals have many similarities. In most cases, the muscles of other animals operate in the same way as do human muscles.

The two main types of muscle are skeletal muscle (also called striated muscle) and smooth muscle. Some animals (sea anemones), for instance, have only striated muscle, while others (for example squid) have both striated and smooth muscle. Humans and other **vertebrates** have striated muscle, smooth muscle and a third type of muscle called cardiac muscle. Cardiac muscle is found only in the heart.

Skeletal muscle

Skeletal muscles are made up of bundles of hundreds or even thousands of long thin muscle cells. Each muscle cell or fibre, is as long as the muscle it is part of and can be several centimetres in length. Unlike other cells, each muscle cell has not one but many **nuclei** along its length. Under the microscope, alternating light and dark bands called striations can be seen in the cells. This is why skeletal muscles are also called striated muscles. Muscle fibres do a great deal of work when they contract. For this reason, muscle cells contain many **mitochondria** – the tiny **organelles** within cells that release energy from **respiration**.

Skeletal muscles make up a large part of our legs, arms, body, neck and face. They help hold the bones of the skeleton together and give the body shape. Whenever you walk, run, jump, laugh, sit up, or turn your head, these muscles are at work moving your body.

Skeletal muscle fibres are held together by tough, flexible connective tissue. This connective tissue extends beyond the muscles to form **tendons**, which attach the muscles to bones. One end of the muscle is attached to a bone that does not move

A magnified photo of striated muscle fibres, showing the bands or striations that give the muscle its name. Magnification approx. x 1200.

when the muscle contracts, while the other end is attached to a bone that is moved by the muscle when it contracts.

Skeletal muscles work in pairs. One muscle of each pair is called the **flexor**. It bends a joint and brings a limb closer to the body. The other muscle, called the **extensor**, does the opposite. For example, the biceps muscle in the front of the upper arm is a flexor. It contracts when you bend your elbow and lifts your hand towards your shoulder. The triceps muscle in the back of the upper arm straightens your elbow and moves your hand away from your shoulder again – it is an extensor.

Smooth muscle

The cells of smooth muscles are smaller than skeletal muscle fibres and have only one nucleus. Smooth muscles are not under conscious control and are sometimes known as involuntary muscles. They follow a rhythmic pattern of contraction and relaxation. Smooth muscles are found in such places as in the walls of the stomach, intestines and blood vessels. The smooth muscles in the walls of the stomach and intestines move food along the digestive system, while the smooth muscles in the walls of blood vessels can contract to regulate the flow of blood.

Cardiac muscle

Cardiac (heart) muscle has characteristics of both skeletal and smooth muscles. Cardiac muscle cells have striations, like skeletal muscle fibres, but like smooth muscle fibres each cardiac muscle cell has only one nucleus and contracts automatically. A group of specialized cells called the sinoatrial node starts up each contraction of the cardiac muscle by giving off a regular electrical pulse. This electrical pulse is the heart's 'pacemaker'. Even if the nerves from the rest of the body to the heart are cut, the heart will keep on beating.

Muscles cannot lengthen and push: they can only contract and produce a pulling force. To push up the weights, this woman is using her chest muscles (pectorals) to pull her arms towards each other, and her triceps muscles on the back of her upper arms, which pull across the elbow joints to straighten them.

Skeletons

A skeleton has three main jobs. First, all but the very smallest animals need some kind of skeleton to support the body and help keep its shape. Second, an animal's skeleton gives protection to delicate organs such as the brain and the heart.

The third job of the skeleton is to help movement. Animals move by contracting and relaxing their muscles, but muscles cannot work without something to pull against. This is what the skeleton provides.

In the animal world there are three basic types of skeleton: **hydrostatic** skeletons, outer skeletons (**exoskeletons**) and inner skeletons (**endoskeletons**).

Hydrostatic skeletons and exoskeletons

Simple animals such as sea anemones have a hydrostatic skeleton. This is a skeleton that works using liquid, which is moved from one part of the body to another by the muscles. Imagine partially filling a balloon with water, then squeezing the water from one end of the balloon to the other. This is similar to what happens when a sea anemone stretches out to feed. Muscles contract to squeeze fluids from the anemone's body into its tentacles. As they fill with fluid, the tentacles stretch out. An earthworm also has a hydrostatic skeleton. It moves by contracting and relaxing a series of fluid-filled compartments along its length.

Insects, spiders and related groups such as crustaceans (crabs and lobsters for example) and centipedes, have a hard outer covering called an exoskeleton. The exoskeleton is rather like a very light, strong suit of armour that protects the animal's internal organs. It is made from a material called chitin. The animal's muscles are attached to the inside wall of the exoskeleton. The exoskeleton is divided into parts called segments, connected to each other by flexible joints. The joints allow the animal to move.

This fish-eating sea anemone uses hydrostatic (liquid) pressure to stretch out its tentacles and grasp its food.

An exoskeleton cannot grow. So as an animal with an exoskeleton grows, the skeleton splits, and the animal sheds its skin (moults). A new exoskeleton forms underneath the old one. The new exoskeleton is soft at first, and the animal can expand and stretch it before it hardens.

Endoskeletons

An endoskeleton, or simply a skeleton, is a rigid internal framework of bone or cartilage. Bone (or occasionally cartilage) forms the framework of the bodies of **vertebrates**, which include fish, reptiles, birds and mammals. Bones support the body and protect its vital organs.

Bone structure

Bone is not a 'dead' tissue. In fact, it is one of the most active tissues of the body. Specialized cells called **osteoblasts** form new bone around themselves by first laying down fibres, then depositing hard crystals of calcium phosphate around them. Bone is constantly being rebuilt. In children, about three per cent (a thirtieth) of the bone in the skeleton is broken down and replaced each year. The rate is much less in adults.

Bones are like banks for minerals, with vital elements such as calcium, phosphorus and sodium being constantly deposited and withdrawn as they are needed by the body. Cells that are embedded in the bone help to control the mineral balance of the body by producing **enzymes** that erode the bone, releasing minerals into the bloodstream as needed.

All bones have blood vessels and nerves. The centre of a bone is hollow and is filled with either red or yellow bone **marrow**. Yellow bone marrow is mostly fat. Red bone marrow is where blood cells are formed. It is found mainly in the bones of the spine, ribs, breastbone and in the ends of the limb bones.

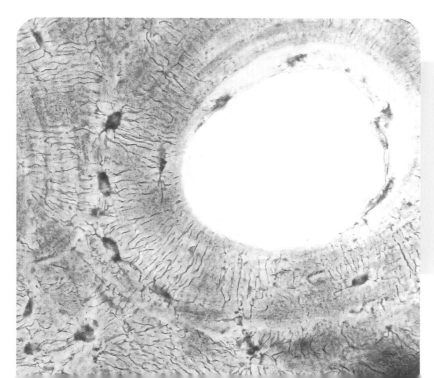

A magnified view of a section of bone. The white circle is a canal (tube) that in the living bone carries nerves and blood vessels. The brown ovals are osteoblasts, the cells that laid down the bone around them. Magnification approx. x 125.

4 Nerve cells

Almost all animals have some type of nervous system. The nervous system is an internal communications network that enables the animal to detect, react and adjust to changes in its environment.

The nervous system is made up of billions of specialized cells called **neurones**. These neurones form a network throughout the body. Information speeds through this network as pulses of electricity – nerve impulses.

Parts of a neurone

A neurone can be divided into three basic parts. The cell body is similar to any other cell and houses the cell's **nucleus** and all the other **organelles** needed for the cell to live and grow. The cell body of the neurone is a centre for receiving and sending nerve impulses.

Stretching out from the cell body of a neurone are a number of long, thin extensions. The longest of them is called the **axon**, or the nerve fibre. The structures commonly called nerves are actually bundles of axons, lying next to one another like wires in a telephone cable.

The axon is specialized to carry nerve impulses from the cell body either to another neurone, or to a muscle or sensory cell. The end of the axon is branched, allowing it to pass on impulses to more than one cell. A single axon may have enough branches to make contact with thousands of other cells. The neurones do not make direct contact with one another, but are separated by a very narrow space, called a **synapse**, across which nerve impulses are transmitted.

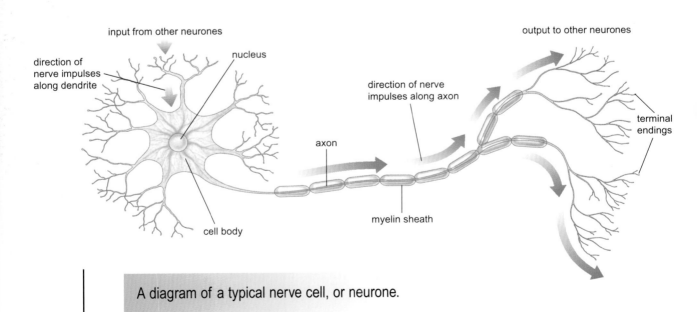

input from other neurones

output to other neurones

direction of
nerve impulses
along dendrite

nucleus

direction of nerve
impulses along axon

terminal
endings

axon

cell body

myelin sheath

A diagram of a typical nerve cell, or neurone.

The other, smaller extensions from the neurone cell body are known as **dendrites**. These are specialized structures for receiving nerve impulses from other neurones. Most neurones have about six main dendrites. They are the paths by which the neurone receives information.

Nerve stretching!

Most axons in the central nervous system are less than a millimetre long. However, the axons that reach from the spinal cord to the muscles in the feet may be up to a metre in length.

Some axons are covered by a white sheath made of fatty material called **myelin**. This insulates the axon along most of its length, except at regular points along the length called nodes. When a nerve impulse travels along a nerve that has a myelin sheath, it 'jumps' from node to node. This makes the impulse travel much more quickly than along a bare nerve fibre.

This photo taken with an electron microscope shows a synapse (joining point) between a nerve fibre (purple) and the body of a nerve cell (yellow). Chemicals released across the synapse pass on the nerve impulse from one cell to the next. Magnification approx. x 10,000.

The nervous system

In **vertebrates**, the nervous system can be divided into two parts: the central nervous system and the peripheral nervous system. The central nervous system is the body's command system, controlling and coordinating the activities of the entire nervous system. The peripheral nervous system carries impulses between the central nervous system and the rest of the body. One part of the peripheral nervous system links to the skeletal muscles, tendons and skin. While another part, sometimes called the autonomic nervous system, carries signals to and from the internal organs, such as the heart and the digestive organs.

The central nervous system

The central nervous system consists of the brain and spinal cord.

The spinal cord is the body's information superhighway. It carries messages back and forth between the brain and the rest of the body.

Nerve impulses travel rapidly up and down the spinal cord through bundles of nerve fibres. Each fibre is covered in a **myelin** sheath. In **vertebrates** the spinal cord threads through a hole or channel that runs down the centre of the vertebral column (the backbone). The vertebrae (the bones of the backbone) protect the spinal cord.

At the top, the spinal cord thickens to form the lowest part of the brain: the **brain stem**. The brain stem contains nerve cells that pass information from the sense organs on to the higher areas of the brain. It is also the area that sets off many reflex reactions (see opposite), and it is the part of the brain that regulates much of the activity of the autonomic nervous system.

cerebrum

cerebellum

spinal cord

A coloured scan of a woman's head, showing a vertical section through the brain. The large cerebrum, the cerebellum and the spinal cord can be seen clearly.

In humans, the main part of the brain is called the **cerebrum**, which consists of two large hemispheres. The cerebrum receives information from the senses, and interprets this information to create a picture of the world around us. The cerebrum also has areas that are responsible for the movement of the different parts of the body, although another part of the brain, the **cerebellum**, is responsible for the fine control of movement. The cerebrum is also the centre of learning and memory.

Circuits and reflexes

Much of the work of the nervous system relies on pathways called neural circuits. A neural circuit is a nerve pathway from the sense organs to the muscles, via the central nervous system. The eyes, ears and other sense organs contain specialized nerve cells called **receptors**, which pick up information from the environment around us. The receptors turn this information into nerve impulses, which travel along **sensory neurones** to neurones in the brain (the cerebrum). The brain analyses the information about the outside world and uses it to decide what action to take. For example, a hunter that sees, smells or hears its prey might decide to move towards it. The brain sends messages to the muscles through other nerve cells called **motor neurones**.

The simplest kind of neural circuit is a reflex – an automatic and involuntary response to a stimulus that doesn't involve conscious thought. Skeletal muscles are sometimes called voluntary muscles because they are usually under conscious control. However, if you were to touch a painfully hot or sharp object your muscles would quickly jerk your hand away without you having to think about it. In a reflex action, impulses follow a simple pathway linking a receptor to a muscle by way of the spinal cord. Many reflexes involve at least one other neurone between the sensory neurone carrying the message into the nervous system, and the motor neurone taking the instruction to the muscles. For example, if you touch a hot object you jerk your hand back but at the same time information is sent to the brain, so that you become aware of what has happened and you know not to touch that object again.

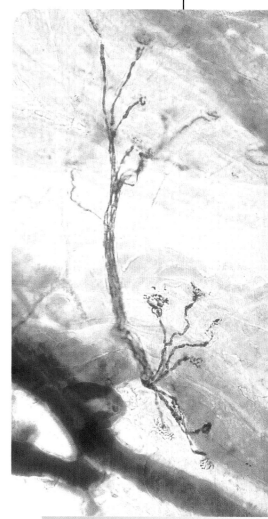

Motor neurones run from the brain and spinal cord to the muscles. Nerve impulses along these neurones stimulate the muscles to contract. This photo shows the branching connections of a motor nerve to muscle tissue. Like the connections between nerves, the connections between nerves and muscles are **synapses**. Magnification approx. x 100.

The senses

The senses are part of the nervous system. They have been described as the receptionists at the nervous system's front door. Through their senses, animals gain information about what is going on inside and outside their bodies. A sensory system consists of three parts: **receptor** cells, which detect a change in the environment, **sensory neurones**, which carry nerve impulses from the receptors to the central nervous system, and an area of the brain that translates the signals from the receptors into a sensation.

Internal and external senses

There are many different kinds of sensory receptor. Internal senses detect chemical and physical changes within the body, for example changes in blood pressure or changes in the size of the stomach. Signals reporting these changes are sent to the brain where they will trigger such feelings as hunger, thirst, tiredness or pain. This constant monitoring helps to keep conditions inside the animal at the optimum for the chemical processes of life to be carried out. It is all part of the cooperation between cells that keeps every cell in the animal healthy.

External senses, such as sight, hearing, touch and taste, receive information about events happening in the outside environment. Receptors near the surface of the body respond to touch, pressure and changes in temperature. The simplest types of receptor are the branched nerve endings in the skin. Chemoreceptors are receptors that detect substances either in the air or in water, depending on where the animal lives. The olfactory (smell) receptors in the human nose are chemoreceptors, as are the taste receptors on the surface of the tongue.

Sense of vision

All living things are sensitive to light. Plants track the sun as it moves across the sky and even **bacteria** can react to a light source. However, it is only more complex animals that have light-sensitive cells (photoreceptors). When light falls on a photoreceptor, it responds by sending out nerve impulses.

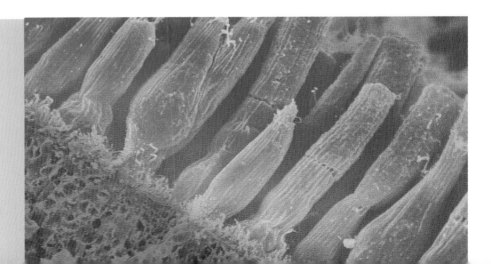

This magnified view of the retina of the human eye shows the different photoreceptors (called rods and cones) within the retina. Magnification approx. x 1200.

Some animals obviously have a better visual sense than others. Earthworms have no eyes but have photoreceptors scattered over their body surface, so they can still react to light. By contrast the eyes of a mammal contain around 125 million photoreceptors, of two kinds: rods and cones. Rod cells are sensitive to dim light and perceive movement at night. Cone cells only work in bright light. There are thought to be three different types of cone cell, each sensitive to a different range of light wavelengths. Therefore they pick up different colours.

Photoreceptors themselves are not enough for an animal to have a true visual sense. Other neurones within the brain or central nervous system are needed to turn the signals from many different photoreceptors into a visual image.

Different worlds

Different animals have different combinations and numbers of receptors. The picture of the world they sense will be different from our own.

In humans, the sense of vision is important. Our vision is quite good, but the eyes of birds of prey, for instance, are much sharper than ours, while many animals have a much wider field of vision than we do.

In other animals smell or hearing may be as important or more important than sight. Your nose has about 5 million olfactory receptors, but a bloodhound's nose has more than 200 million. Bats have very poor vision, but a sharp sense of hearing. They make strings of high-pitched sounds, and from the echoes that bounce back from the objects around them, they can build up a 'sound picture' of their environment.

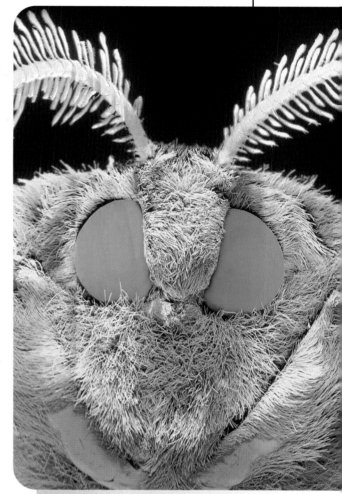

Male moths are so sensitive to a smell released by females of the same species that they can pick up the scent several kilometres away. The long feathery antennae of this silk moth carry millions of olfactory receptors. Magnification approx. x 20.

The picture of the world that a bee has, or a bat, is very different to our own. For example, to a bee, which has photoreceptors that are sensitive to ultraviolet light, a flower has patterns that show where the nectar is.

5 Chemical messengers

The activities of the multicelled animal are not only controlled by its nervous system. Cells also respond to changes in their surroundings by taking up and releasing various chemicals. These chemical responses have to be coordinated in some way to ensure that the millions or even billions of cells that make up the animal's body are all working together. This is done through the use of signalling molecules, called **hormones**, that travel through the blood from one part of the body to another.

Hormones

The word hormone comes from a Greek word that means 'to set in motion'. Hormones control body activities such as growth, development and reproduction. For example, the metamorphosis of a caterpillar into a butterfly is regulated by hormones. **Vertebrates**, especially mammals, all have very nearly the same hormones doing the same jobs. For this reason, hormones secreted by other animals can be used to treat people who do not produce sufficient amounts of these hormones themselves. For example, millions of people have diabetes, a disorder caused by a deficiency in the hormone insulin. Up until the 1980s doctors treated the condition by giving diabetics insulin obtained from animals such as pigs. Today, genetically altered **bacteria** are used to manufacture human insulin.

The endocrine glands

Most hormones in the human body are produced by organs called **endocrine glands**. The major endocrine glands include the two adrenal glands, the pituitary gland, the four parathyroid glands, the sex glands (**ovaries** in the female, **testes** in the male) and the thyroid gland. A few hormones are produced by endocrine cells found in organs such as the pancreas and the stomach. Hormones produced in the endocrine glands are released into the blood, which carries them throughout the body.

This photograph shows the effects that a hormone called growth hormone can have on height. The woman, French actress Mimie Mathy, suffers from dwarfism (too little growth hormone). The man is normal height.

Hormones can be grouped according to the jobs they do. Metabolic hormones, for example, regulate the various steps in **metabolism**: the release of energy from food and the growth of new cells.

The endocrine cells in the stomach and small intestine produce hormones that regulate digestion. These control the production of **enzymes** that break down food into substances that can be used by the body. Once the digested food molecules have been absorbed into the bloodstream, other hormones control their use in the body. For example the hormone insulin, which has already been mentioned, is produced by the pancreas. It causes **glucose** in the bloodstream to be converted into glycogen, a **carbohydrate** that is stored in the liver and in muscle cells. Another hormone, glucagon, is also secreted by the pancreas. It causes the liver to stop making glycogen and start converting it back into glucose. In this way the pancreas regulates the amount of sugar (which the cells use for energy) in the blood.

Coordinated action

The nervous system and the endocrine system act together as a unit. The sense organs gather information on changes in the environment, which they pass on to the brain through the nervous system. The brain uses this information to decide if any action needs to be taken: if so, it triggers a response.

For example, in times of danger or excitement, signals from part of the autonomic nervous system prepare the body to face a stressful situation. Nerve signals trigger the release of the stress hormones adrenaline and noradrenaline from the adrenal glands. These substances have several different effects. For example, adrenaline increases the heart rate, and speeds up the release of energy from food in the muscles.

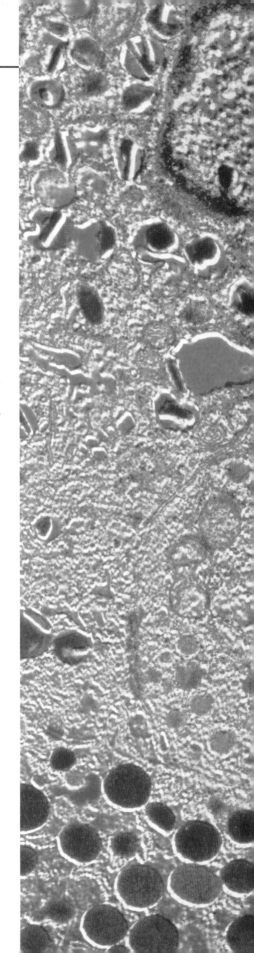

This magnified view shows cells, of the islets of Langerhans, in the pancreas. The green cells at the top produce the hormone insulin, while the pink cells on the bottom produce glucagon. Magnification approx. x 3000.

6 Regulation and control

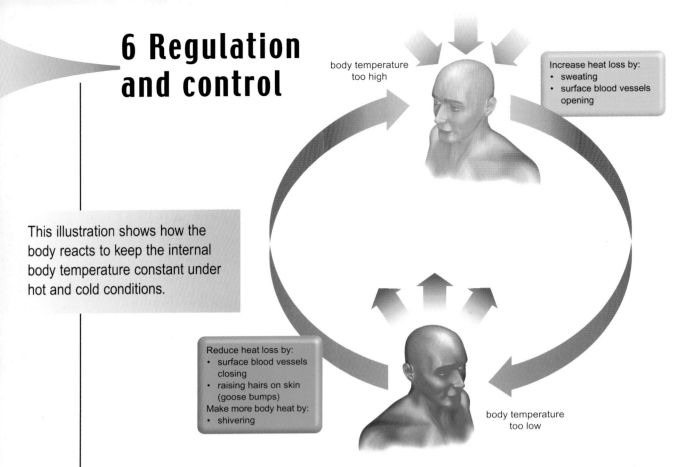

body temperature too high

Increase heat loss by:
• sweating
• surface blood vessels opening

This illustration shows how the body reacts to keep the internal body temperature constant under hot and cold conditions.

Reduce heat loss by:
• surface blood vessels closing
• raising hairs on skin (goose bumps)
Make more body heat by:
• shivering

body temperature too low

A healthy animal has to maintain conditions at the best level for its cells to work efficiently. A cell's **enzymes**, for example, work best within a temperature range of between 30 and 40 °C.

At temperatures higher than this, the enzymes begin to break down, cell processes cease and the organism dies. Controlling temperature, the supply of water and the supply of **nutrients** to the cells is crucial. In order to stay alive your cells, or those of any other animal, must be brought all the nutrients they need, and the waste products of the cells have to be removed.

The body's internal senses keep track of the the changing conditions inside the body. If the internal environment is out of balance, it triggers responses such as shivering, hunger, thirst, production of water-retaining **hormones** and so on. Keeping a stable set of conditions inside an animal's body is called **homeostasis**. All of the parts of the animal work together to maintain conditions.

Environmental control

An animal often has to make internal adjustments in response to changes in the outside environment such as changes in temperature or humidity. These changes in the outside world set off homeostatic reflexes. One example is what happens when you step out from a cool house into the full heat of the sun. It is absolutely vital that the cells of your body do not get overheated, and homeostatic mechanisms ensure that this does not happen.

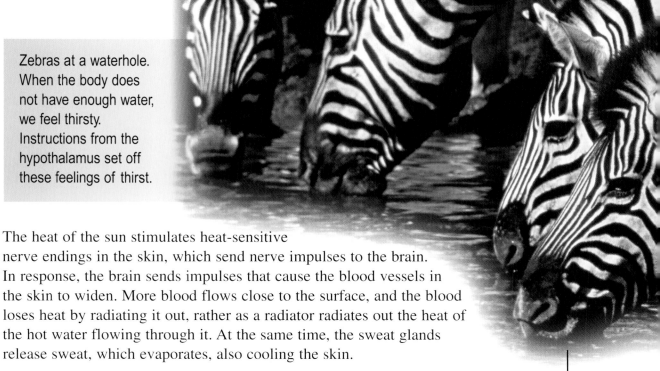

Zebras at a waterhole. When the body does not have enough water, we feel thirsty. Instructions from the hypothalamus set off these feelings of thirst.

The heat of the sun stimulates heat-sensitive nerve endings in the skin, which send nerve impulses to the brain. In response, the brain sends impulses that cause the blood vessels in the skin to widen. More blood flows close to the surface, and the blood loses heat by radiating it out, rather as a radiator radiates out the heat of the hot water flowing through it. At the same time, the sweat glands release sweat, which evaporates, also cooling the skin.

All these changes in the body happen without you having to think about it at all. You couldn't make these sort of changes in your body by thinking, nor could you stop them from happening. The whole process is automatic.

Hunger and thirst

Everyone recognizes the feelings of hunger: rumbling of the stomach, restlessness, and perhaps a weak or tired feeling. The body has plenty of ways to tell us that we need to eat! Normally, an animal eats just enough to satisfy its needs, and its body weight remains about the same. You will almost never see a fat wild animal. A part of the brain called the hypothalamus contains **receptors** that are sensitive to the amount of sugar in the blood, and it is responsible for keeping our blood sugar levels in balance. If the hypothalamus is damaged, the result can be either excessive eating or complete loss of appetite.

When we are thirsty, we experience a dry feeling in the mouth. This is because the mouth is producing less saliva in order to conserve the body's supply of water. The dryness in your mouth makes you want to drink.

The hypothalamus also plays an important part in regulating the amount of water present in the body. Cells in the hypothalamus called osmoreceptors are sensitive to changes in the composition of the blood. If the amount of water in the blood falls, this stimulates the osmoreceptors. A hormone called ADH (antidiuretic hormone) is released, and it acts to reduce the amount of urine produced. This conserves the body's water. When you drink, the water content of the blood is restored to normal levels and the production of ADH falls once more.

27

Waste management

An animal cell exists in a watery world. The cell is surrounded by a weak chemical solution that fills the spaces between cells. Cells take in substances they need from this fluid, and pass waste material into it – for example waste products of chemical reactions, excess water and salts, and **hormones** that have done their job. If these waste products were allowed to build up, they would quickly become harmful. All animals need a way to get rid of these waste products in order to keep healthy. The process of doing so is called **excretion**.

One important waste product is carbon dioxide. This is formed when sugars or other **carbohydrates** are broken down to release energy. Carbon dioxide can be transported easily by the blood. It travels through the bloodstream to the lungs, where it is breathed out.

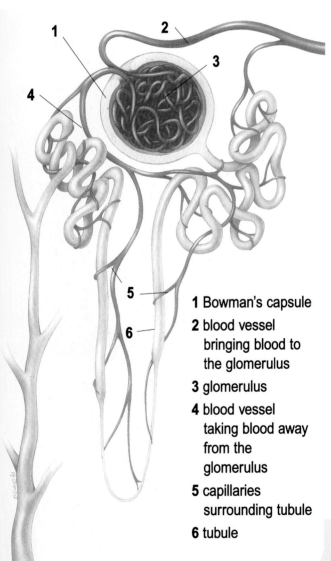

1 Bowman's capsule
2 blood vessel bringing blood to the glomerulus
3 glomerulus
4 blood vessel taking blood away from the glomerulus
5 capillaries surrounding tubule
6 tubule

The urinary system

Other waste products cannot be removed from the body as simply as carbon dioxide. In mammals, special organs called the kidneys are responsible for excretion of these and other wastes.

The kidneys are part of the urinary system, which plays an important part in regulating the amount of water and dissolved substances in the body. The kidneys filter the blood removing unwanted substances such as salts. Some of the main waste products are nitrogen-containing compounds formed by the breakdown of **proteins**.

Blood arrives in the kidneys in a blood vessel called the renal artery. Inside the kidney this artery divides many times until it forms a network of tiny capillaries, through which the red blood cells squeeze in single file. The capillaries coil into tiny little bundles, each of which is called a **glomerulus**. Each glomerulus is almost entirely surrounded by a cup-shaped structure called a **Bowman's capsule**.

This illustration shows a single unit of the kidney – a glomerulus, Bowman's capsule, tubule and surrounding capillaries. The whole unit is called a **nephron**.

Blood pressure inside the glomerulus causes some of the liquid part of the blood (the **plasma**) to leak out through the capillary walls. Red blood cells and large protein molecules in the blood do not escape because they are too big. The fluid that does pass through is mainly water with salts, **glucose**, and nitrogen compounds dissolved in it.

The fluid that leaks from the capillaries collects in the Bowman's capsule and trickles down a looping **tubule**. The capillaries themselves form a network around the tubule. As fluid passes through the tubule, substances needed by the body are reabsorbed into the capillaries. All of the glucose is reabsorbed, along with much of the water and some salts. Excess salt passes on down the tubule, along with some water and the nitrogen compounds. Eventually this waste material ends up in the bladder, where it is stored until it can be passed out of the body as urine.

Osmosis

Water flows in and out of a cell by **osmosis** – the movement of water across a **membrane**. Where two solutions are separated by a cell membrane, or any other partially permeable membrane, water flows from the more concentrated solution to the less concentrated one. Substances can also be pumped across a cell membrane by proteins embedded in it (this is called active transport). Active transport can be used to move chemicals from a region of low concentration to one of higher concentration. Unlike osmosis this requires energy from respiration.

The kangaroo rat lives in the desert, where there is very little water available. It has a specialized kidney, containing nephrons with very long tubules, to save extra water.

7 Feeding and digestion

All animals need to eat food. The **nutrients** in food give the animal the raw materials needed to build new cells and repair cell parts. Food is also the 'fuel' an animal needs to power activity in its cells.

An animal's food contains **proteins**, **carbohydrates**, **lipids** (fats) and other compounds similar to those that make up the body of the animal itself. However, the molecules in the food are mostly too big to be absorbed directly by the animal's cells. First they have to be broken down into simpler substances, such as simple sugars from the carbohydrates and **amino acids** (the building blocks of proteins), which can be absorbed into the blood. The sugars, amino acids and other small molecules can then be used as a source of energy, or as building blocks to assemble new cell parts.

The digestive system is responsible for taking nutrients in and making them available to the body's cells. The digestive system has five jobs to do:
• to break up, mix and move the food along
• to produce and release digestive **enzymes**
• to break down the food into molecules small enough to be absorbed
• to provide a large surface area so these nutrients can be absorbed into the blood for transport to the rest of the body
• to remove the undigested remains of the food.

A balanced diet

All animals need a similar mix of basic nutrients in their food. Some animals can make certain nutrients that others cannot, but generally a balanced diet consists of a mixture of **carbohydrates**, **proteins**, **lipids** and **vitamins**.

This flowchart shows how food is broken down into different nutrients, which can then be used in different ways in the cells.

Proteins — enzyme action — amino acids — absorption — amino acids

Carbohydrates — enzyme action — simple sugars — absorption — sugars

Lipids — emulsification (fat droplets broken up) — tiny fat droplets — enzyme action — simpler molecules — new fats built — new fats

small intestine

blood vessel

Carbohydrates are the main energy source for animal cells. Large carbohydrates such as starch cannot be directly absorbed. They need to be broken down to smaller sugars such as **glucose**. Glucose is the sugar that is most readily absorbed and used by cells. No particular carbohydrates are essential, but an animal deprived of carbohydrate altogether will eventually die.

Proteins are essential parts of a cell. Large protein molecules are made inside cells from smaller amino acids that are obtained from the diet. Animal cells use around 20 different amino acids. For most animals, half of these amino acids are essential. This means that the animals cannot make them from other chemicals, so unless they are in its diet the animal will become ill and die.

Lipids include fats and similar compounds. Lipids are an essential part of cell **membranes**, and droplets of fat are stored in the **cytoplasm** as a source of energy. Lipids can be made from a range of simpler compounds. Many animals need little or no fat in their diet, as lipids can be made inside cells from both proteins and carbohydrates. However, compounds known as essential fatty acids cannot be made by some animals and have to be eaten in food.

Vitamins are a varied group of molecules that are needed for building larger molecules or for taking part in chemical reactions in cells. Plants can make all the vitamins they need, but animals must get them from their diet.

Some **minerals**, such as calcium for building bones and iron for making red blood cells are also needed in the diet.

Finally, all living cells need water. As much as 95 per cent of the body weight of some animals is water. Water is lost from the lungs through breathing, and in the urine. In some mammals, water is also lost through sweating. This water loss has to be replaced if the animal is to stay healthy. Water can be replaced by eating as well as drinking. A healthy adult human will get nearly as much water from food as from drinking.

Fresh fruit and vegetables, such as those shown here, supply our vitamins and minerals. Some people supplement these sources by taking vitamin pills.

The digestive tract

There are just about as many different methods of feeding as there are different types of animal. Some eat very small food particles, others eat larger things. Some scrape and bore into their food, others catch it and chew it before swallowing. Some feed on the fluids produced by plants or other animals.

Large animals need a digestive tube, or tract, where food can be processed and broken down into usable components. The first stages in the digestive process take place in the mouth. Here the food can be crushed and ground up into small pieces that will give the digestive **enzymes** a greater surface area to work on. When the food has been sufficiently chewed, it is pushed back by the tongue and swallowed. A tube called the **oesophagus** carries the food to the stomach.

The stomach

The stomach is one of the most important organs of the digestive system. It has three main jobs. First, it mixes and stores food arriving from the oesophagus. Second, it produces digestive juices, containing enzymes, that dissolve and begin the breakdown of the food. Third, it acts as a sort of holding area for food, which is then released slowly into the small intestine.

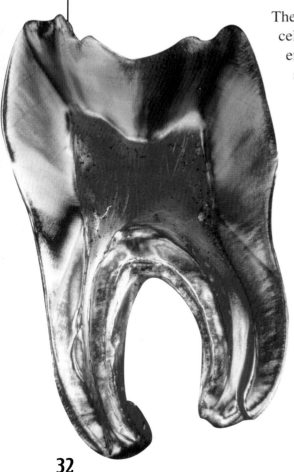

The lining of the stomach has a great many glandular cells that produce gastric fluid. This fluid contains an enzyme called pepsin, which breaks up **proteins** into smaller molecules. The stomach also produces hydrochloric acid, which provides the acid conditions in which pepsin works best. It also helps to kill many **bacteria** and other micro-organisms in the food. The stomach produces about two litres of gastric fluid every day.

The stomach has bands of muscle in its walls. Waves of contraction and relaxation, called peristalsis, pass through the walls of the stomach, mixing and churning the stomach contents. These waves get stronger as they get nearer to the base of the stomach.

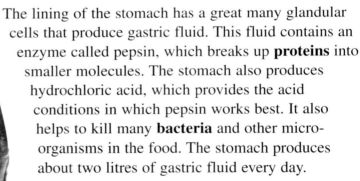

A cross-section through a human tooth, taken using polarized light. Teeth are used to grind and cut up food before it travels to the stomach.

Cow's world

Herbivores, such as cows, eat large amounts of grass and other plant material. The main **carbohydrate** in this food is cellulose, which the animals themselves cannot digest, but a cow's stomach contains millions of bacteria that produce a cellulose-digesting enzyme. The cellulose is broken down by these bacteria, releasing **nutrients** that the cow can use.

A great many other micro-organisms are also found in the cow's stomach. Some of these are eaten by single-celled creatures called **protistans**, which also live in the stomach. The protistans in their turn are digested in the cow's small intestine. This gives a protein boost to the cow's otherwise low-protein diet.

The small intestine

In mammals, the small intestine is where most of the process of digestion and absorption takes place. The lining of the small intestine produces intestinal juice, pancreatic juice enters from the pancreas and bile enters the small intestine from the gall bladder in the liver. All these juices are rich in enzymes that are involved in the digestive process.

Covering the internal surface of the small intestine are masses of small, finger-like projections called villi. Each of these villi is itself covered with thousands of even tinier projections called microvilli. Together the villi and microvilli increase enormously the surface area available for absorbing the products of digestion. Immediately beneath the **epithelium** of the small intestine there is a network of small blood capillaries. **Nutrients** diffuse into these capillaries from the intestine.

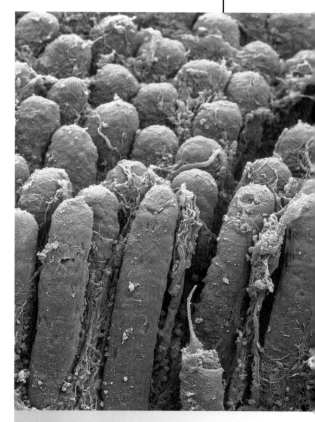

A photo taken with a scanning electron microscope showing the villi of the small intestine. Magnification approx. x 100.

The large intestine

Material not absorbed by the small intestine passes into the large intestine, or colon. In humans and carnivores, little digestion takes place in the large intestine. Its main purpose is to absorb water and to compress the undigested waste into a compact mass, which will passes out of the body through the anus. In many herbivores (such as rabbits and horses), however, the large intestine contains millions of cellulose-digesting bacteria.

8 Circulation and respiration

Once food has been digested and absorbed, it has to be transported to all the cells of the body. Blood is the body's transport system. The blood carries **nutrients** to the cells – as well as oxygen, which the cells need to get energy from food. The blood carries waste products away from the cells: nitrogen-containing compounds and salts to be **excreted** by the kidneys, and carbon dioxide to the lungs. **Hormones** also travel in the blood from the **endocrine glands** to the places where they act.

About half the volume of blood consists of blood cells. The rest is a yellowish liquid, the **plasma**. Most of the cells are red blood cells, which look like discs dented on each side. They are red because they contain a pigment called haemoglobin. Oxygen binds to haemoglobin, and this is how it is transported in the blood. The blood also contains white blood cells, which are an important part of the immune system (the body's defence system against disease).

Circulation

Blood travels through a huge network of blood vessels that extends to all parts of the body. The central part of this network is the heart. The heart is a muscular pump, that pushes blood around two separate circuits. One circuit flows through the lungs, where the blood picks up oxygen and gets rid of carbon dioxide. This is called the pulmonary circuit. The second circuit takes the oxygen-filled blood to all parts of the body, where the cells take up the oxygen in exchange for waste carbon dioxide. This is called the systemic circuit.

Arteries carry blood from the heart to the rest of the body. An artery has an inner lining of **epithelial** cells, the endothelium. This forms a smooth surface, allowing the blood to flow easily through the artery. Next comes a middle layer of smooth muscle, and an outer layer of fibrous and elastic tissue. Arteries are very strong. They have to be to withstand the pressure of the blood leaving the heart. As arteries reach the body's tissues they divide into smaller vessels called arterioles. Arterioles are similar to arteries but have more smooth muscle in their walls. This muscle can contract, allowing the arterioles to either close down or open up, depending on how much blood needs to flow to a particular part of the body.

This magnified photo shows blood capillaries carrying blood to human muscle cells. Magnification approx. x 120.

The arterioles branch again and again, eventually forming the tiniest of the blood vessels – the capillaries. The walls of a capillary consist of just a single layer of endothelium, one cell thick. These vessels are so small that red blood cells have to pass along them in single file. No cell in the body is more than 0.2 millimetre away from a capillary, and most are much closer. Plasma passes relatively easily out of blood capillaries, leaking out through gaps between the cells in the walls. This provides a means of exchanging substances between the body cells and the blood. When plasma passes out of the blood into tissues it is called tissue fluid. All of the body's cells are bathed in this fluid. We have already seen how maintaining the composition of this fluid is an essential part of keeping the cells healthy.

Red blood cells cannot pass out of the capillaries, but white blood cells can squeeze through the gaps between cells. The red blood cells exchange the oxygen they carry with the tissue fluid, allowing it to reach the cells. Carbon dioxide waste from the cells diffuses into the capillaries. Most of it is carried dissolved in the plasma, but some links up with the haemoglobin in the red blood cells.

About 90 per cent of fluid that leaks from the capillaries eventually gets back in. The capillaries join up once more to form larger vessels called venules, which combine to form veins. The job of veins is to return blood to the heart. The structure of a vein is much the same as that of an artery but the muscle layer is much thinner. Veins do not need to have thick walls like arteries, because the pressure of the returning blood is much lower. Along the inside of the veins at regular intervals there are valves, which allow blood to flow towards the heart but not away from it.

Better red than dead

A single cubic millimetre of human blood contains about 5 million red blood cells, each of which carries around 250 million molecules of haemoglobin. Each haemoglobin molecule can carry four molecules of oxygen, so a single red blood cell can carry up to a billion oxygen molecules. Red blood cells are unusual in that they contain no **nucleus** and no **mitochondria**. This maximises the space available for haemoglobin and therefore the amount of oxygen each cell can carry.

This electron micrograph shows red blood cells passing into a small blood vessel. Magnification approx. x 2000.

Breathing

The energy that body cells need is released from food by a series of chemical reactions called **respiration**. Respiration takes place inside the cell, in **organelles** called **mitochondria**. The process needs oxygen and produces carbon dioxide as a waste material, so all animals need to get oxygen to their cells from the outside environment, and get rid of waste carbon dioxide. This process is called gas exchange. It takes place in different ways in different animals.

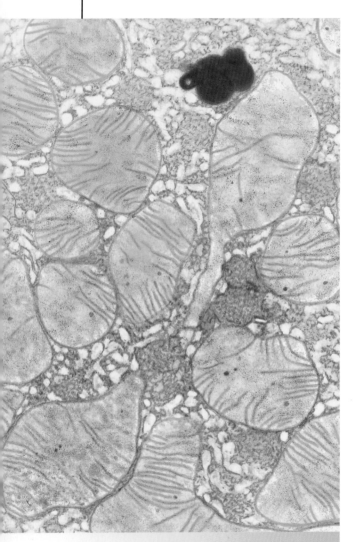

Mitochondria (shown here in green) are the energy factories of a cell. The chemical reactions of respiration take place in the mitochondria. The process releases energy that the cell can use to grow and repair itself. Magnification approx. x 46,000.

Gills

Most water has oxygen dissolved in it. Water that contains no oxygen cannot support life (apart from special types of bacteria). Animals that live in water, such as fish, have specialized organs called **gills** for gas exchange.

Gills are adapted so that there is a constant flow of water over the inner surface of gill. This surface is highly folded to give it a large area, and a great many small blood capillaries run just beneath. The blood that flows into the gills is returning from the body via the heart, so it has very little oxygen but high levels of carbon dioxide. The water flowing through the gills has more oxygen, so some of it passes out of the water and into the blood. On the other hand the blood contains more carbon dioxide, so this passes out of the blood and into the water.

Gills cannot work out of the water because the folds of the gills stick together if water is not kept flowing through them. This is why a fish will suffocate if removed from water, even though there is much more oxygen in the air than there is dissolved in water.

Air tubes and lungs

Air has much more oxygen in it than water, and the levels of carbon dioxide are very low. Different land-living animals have different ways of getting oxygen from the air.

Insects have a network of branching hollow tubes called tracheae that run throughout the body. The tracheae connect to small holes called spiracles on the body surface. Movement of the insect's body and its flight muscles help to move gases in and out of the tracheae. Oxygen moves slowly from the tracheae into the insect's circulatory system, while carbon dioxide moves the other way. The system of tracheae is not a very efficient method of gas exchange. This is one of the reasons why insects do not grow very big.

All mammals breathe by means of lungs. Like gills, lungs have a large surface area across which the exchange of oxygen and carbon dioxide can take place.

Air enters the body through the nose or mouth and passes down into the **trachea**, or windpipe. The trachea splits into two smaller air passages called bronchi, one leading to each lung. Inside the lung the bronchi divide into smaller and smaller airways, which finally end up in tiny air sacs called **alveoli**. These look rather like microscopic bunches of grapes. Each of these alveoli is lined with a moist **epithelium**, just a single cell thick. Running around the alveoli is a network of thin-walled capillaries.

Blood entering the lungs has little oxygen but is full of carbon dioxide. Carbon dioxide leaves the blood and is breathed out into the air. Oxygen enters the blood and binds to haemoglobin molecules in the red blood cells. It takes less than half a second for a red blood cell to load up with a billion oxygen molecules. From this point it is the job of the circulatory system to move the oxygen to the cells of the body.

Take a deep breath

There are about 300 million alveoli in each of your lungs. In adult humans the total surface area available for gas exchange in the lungs is about 70 square metres – enough to cover a tennis court.

A magnified cross-section through a group of alveoli, showing the tiny air sacs. Magnification approx. x 400.

9 Fighting infection

All animals have some sort of defence against disease. In **vertebrates**, the immune system is the body's defence force. The immune system destroys disease-causing micro-organisms, such as **bacteria** and **viruses**, that attack the animal's cells. Some of the body's defences are ready at all times, and are non-specific (they are activated by any micro-organism). Other defences are more specific and are only activated by particular disease-causing micro-organisms.

Front-line defences

Front-line defences are always in place – ready to deal with infection whenever it occurs. The first line of defence against disease is the skin. In many animals the skin acts as a physical barrier, stopping the great majority of disease-causing organisms from getting into the body. Other areas, such as the lining of the intestines and the throat, are protected by **membranes** covered with a layer of **mucus**. This mucus contains **enzymes** such as lysozyme, which can destroy bacteria.

If micro-organisms manage to get through the body's outer defences (for example through a cut or a sore), they soon come up against the white blood cells. Some of these cells, called **phagocytes**, deal with the invaders by engulfing and digesting them (a process called phagocytosis). Other specialized white blood cells, called **mast cells**, release a chemical called histamine into the infected area. This is what causes the symptoms of pain, swelling and redness around a wound. The redness is caused by the movement of more blood into the infected area. White blood cells escape from the blood vessels and move towards the site of the infection, guided by the presence of the histamine. Once there, they help to destroy the invading micro-organisms.

Specific responses

Another part of the immune system mounts specific attacks against particular organisms. When a micro-organism enters the body, the immune system identifies it as an outsider and launches a response against it. Millions of specialized white blood cells circulate through the body in search of foreign cells and molecules. The surface of each of these white

Phagocytes are white blood cells that engulf and digest foreign cells. In this picture a phagocyte engulfs a yeast cell. Magnification approx. x 6500.

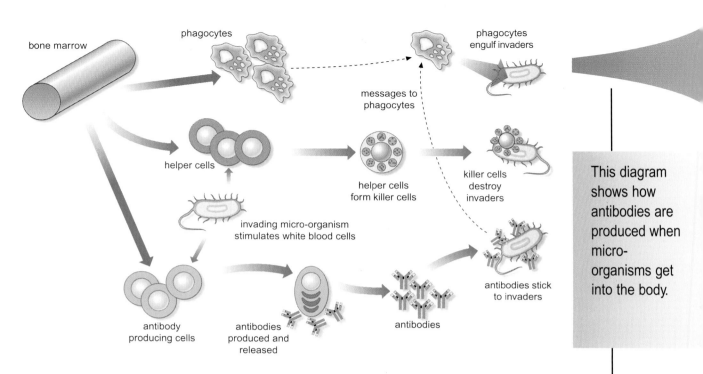

bone marrow

phagocytes

phagocytes
engulf invaders

messages to
phagocytes

helper cells

helper cells
form killer cells

killer cells
destroy
invaders

invading micro-organism
stimulates white blood cells

antibodies stick
to invaders

antibody
producing cells

antibodies
produced and
released

antibodies

This diagram
shows how
antibodies are
produced when
micro-
organisms get
into the body.

blood cells carries **proteins** called **antibodies**. Different cells carry different antibodies, and each antibody recognizes a specific foreign substance called an **antigen**.

When a white blood cell comes across an antigen it recognizes, it rapidly divides to produce a great many identical cells, each of which releases free antibodies into the bloodstream. The antibodies attach themselves to the invader and send chemical signals to the phagocytes. The phagocytes then engulf the invaders and digest them.

The first time it meets a new invader, the body needs time to produce antibodies. However, if the invader returns, the body 'remembers' the micro-organism from the first time, and it mounts a much more rapid and effective defence. This is what is meant when we say that an animal has become **immune** to an infection. It is why we only catch diseases such as German measles once.

Antibodies are effective against bacteria and many other disease-causing micro-organisms. But for **viruses**, the very smallest disease causing organism, antibodies work only in the bloodstream: they are ineffective against viruses once they have entered the body's cells. In this case, cells called helper cells recognize changes in the invaded cell caused by the viruses. They then activate killer cells that lock on to the invaded cells and destroy them.

Allergies

Sometimes the immune system goes into action against a harmless substance. A familiar example of this can be seen, and heard, every spring and summer when some people start sneezing as pollen grains are released from flowering plants. A sufferer's immune system treats the proteins projecting from the surface of pollen grains as antigens, and launches a defence that causes a runny nose, itchy eyes, and a lot of sneezing.

10 Reproduction

One of the definitions of a living thing is that it reproduces. When animals reproduce, they always produce **offspring** that will eventually look more or less like their parents. A cow would never give birth to an ostrich, or an alligator to a dandelion. The key to how animals can reproduce themselves, generation after generation, is in the genetic material in the **nucleus** of every animal cell.

Hydra are simple animals that can reproduce by sexual or asexual methods. In asexual reproduction a young hydra buds off from the parent. Magnification approx. x 800.

The genetic material is a set of instructions, that contains all the information needed to make a complete organism. The instructions are contained in the structure of a molecule called DNA, or deoxyribonucleic acid. Each 'instruction' is a section of DNA called a gene, which is the template for building a single **protein**. Because proteins, in the form of **enzymes**, control all the reactions in a cell, they control the development of the cell.

During reproduction a copy of all of an animal's genes are passed on to the next generation. In the simplest form of reproduction, a single organism passes on a copy of its genetic material to its offspring: the offspring are genetically identical to their parents. This type of reproduction is called **asexual reproduction**. Many of the simplest animals reproduce this way most of the time, and some more complex animals reproduce asexually at certain stages in their life.

Sexual reproduction

Sexual reproduction involves two organisms, both of which contribute genes to their offspring. In most animals there are two distinct sexes, male and female.

Sexual reproduction involves the joining of a sex cell (a **gamete**) from a male animal with a gamete from a female of the same kind. Gametes contain genes from the parents but each gamete has only half the number of **chromosomes** as the parent. To make a complete organism the gametes must combine – this is called **fertilization**.

Female mammals have a pair of reproductive organs called **ovaries** where the female gametes (egg cells) are produced. Within the ovary are structures called follicles, which give rise to the eggs. In humans, usually one follicle ripens at a time and releases an egg, but other mammals release several eggs. The elephant shrew sheds over a hundred eggs at a time.

Once released, the egg or eggs pass along a tube called the **oviduct**. The wall of the oviduct is lined with **epithelial** cells that have many **cilia**. These create a current that carries the egg towards the **uterus**, where the egg will develop and grow if it is fertilized.

For fertilization to happen the egg must meet a male gamete, or **sperm**. Sperm are made in a pair of organs called **testes**, which are part of the male reproductive system.

Fertilization

In mammals, fertilization takes place in the oviduct, inside the female's body. For this to happen, the male has to release sperm into an opening in the female's body that gives access to the eggs (in humans this opening is called the **vagina**).

Of the several hundred million sperm cells that enter the female, only a few hundred will get as far as the oviduct, and only one of these will fertilize the egg. The nucleus of the sperm enters the egg cell and fuses (joins) with the nucleus of the egg. This is the moment of fertilization. In mammals, once fertilization has taken place, the egg divides to form a ball of cells, which travels down the oviduct to the uterus. Here it implants itself in the uterus lining, which grows around it.

An egg cell and a sperm cell are quite different from one another. A sperm cell looks like a microscopic tadpole. The 'head' contains the chromosomes and the 'tail' propels it towards the egg. The egg is much bigger than the sperm. As well as a set of chromosomes it has the organelles and nutrients needed to begin cell division once it is fertilized.

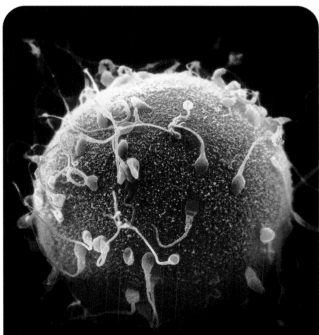

This electron microscope photo shows a human egg cell surrounded by sperm cells. Magnification approx. x 1000.

Development

Development in animals begins as soon as an egg cell is fertilized. The fertilized cell begins to divide repeatedly to form an **embryo**. At first the embryo consists of a ball of identical cells, but soon the cells start to become different from one another.

This scanning electron micrograph shows the early stages of the development of a human embryo. Magnification approx. x 900.

Immediately after fertilization, the embryo consists of a single cell, the fertilized egg. It then divides into two cells, then four, eight, and so on. At this stage the egg **cytoplasm** is simply being divided up among a growing number of smaller cells, each with their own **nucleus**. There is no cell growth and the embryo stays at about the same size. This stage is called cleavage.

Eventually a fluid-filled, hollow ball of cells forms. The frantic pace of cell division slackens off and the embryo enters the next stage of development.

Germ layers

The next stage is marked by some major reorganization as the hollow ball of cells rearranges itself into two or three distinct layers, called germ layers. The cells that develop from these layers will form all of the tissues and organs in the adult organism.

After the germ layers have formed, cell division continues. But now, the cells that are produced are not all the same. Each part of the embryo produces cells that are specialized for the job they will do in the grown animal. This is the beginning of organ formation.

Once the different organs are fully formed, in the final stage of development they grow in size and take on the specialized functions they will perform throughout the life of the organism.

Nourishing and protecting

The growing embryo is helpless, and has to be protected as it grows. The embryo also needs to be fed, as it cannot get food for itself. Different methods of protecting and feeding the developing embryo have evolved in different animals.

In almost all mammals and some reptiles, the embryo grows inside the female's body after fertilization. In mammals, the embryo grows in the **uterus**.

One group of mammals, the marsupials (for example kangaroos and koalas), give birth to extremely underdeveloped young. The young continue their development in a pouch on the mother's body, where they feed on the mother's milk. Other mammals, however, give birth to **offspring** that are well developed. While the embryo of this type of mammal is developing in the uterus, it receives nourishment from the mother's blood through a specialized organ called the **placenta**. These mammals are called placentals. Marsupials do not have placentas.

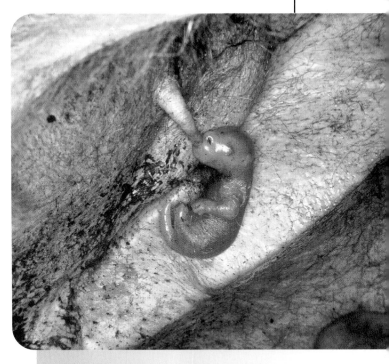

Photograph of very young kangaroo inside the mother's pouch.

The placenta is attached closely to the lining of the uterus and is connected to the embryo by a tube called the **umbilical cord**. Blood vessels in the placenta are very close to blood vessels in the uterus, so that nutrients and oxygen can cross from the mother's blood to that of the embryo. In the same way, carbon dioxide and other waste materials pass from the embryo's blood into the mother's. There is no physical contact between the mother's blood system and that of the embryo.

Birth

Once the embryo is fully formed, and has grown enough to survive outside the uterus, the mother gives birth to her young. The number of young varies from species to species. Domestic pigs may produce litters of up to 16 piglets, whereas elephants and humans tend to have one offspring at a time. The length of the pregnancy also varies from species to species. After 21 days a rat gives birth to small, naked young with closed eyes and ears that obviously still have some developing to do. Guinea pigs give birth after 68 days to young that are well developed and look like miniature adults. Birth is the first step towards an independent life for the new multicelled animal. The next generation is on its way.

The animal kingdom

Animals are multicellular **eukaryotes** that obtain their energy from organic substances produced by other organisms. They develop from the fusion of two **gametes**, one from each parent, although many can also multiply **asexually**. There are many and various kinds of animals but they can be generally classified as those with backbones (**vertebrates**) and those without backbones (**invertebrates**) – examples are listed in the table below:

Classification		Features	Examples
Invertebrates (animals without backbones)	Coelenterates	water-living animals, mostly marine; simple bodies with tentacles and stinging cells, living singly or in colonies, attached to rocks and other surfaces, or free-floating	jellyfish, sea anemonies, coral
	Platyhelminthes	most are parasites of other animals but some live in fresh water; generally have long flat bodies	flatworms, tapeworms, blood flukes
	Nematodes	most are parasites of plants or animals, some live in soil; bodies are long and threadlike	roundworms
	Annelids	most live in water, some in soil; worms with long segmented bodies	earthworms, leeches, ragworms
	Molluscs	most are water-living, some found on the seashore or on land; soft, unsegmented bodies, sometimes protected by a shell	slugs, snails, squid, shellfish
	Echinoderms	marine animals often with tough spiny skin; body plan is based on a five part pattern	starfish
	Arthropods	animals with segmented bodies and jointed legs, protected by a hard outer exoskeleton	
	Crustaceans	mainly water-dwelling, shield-like covering protects the front part of the body; two pairs of antennae, at least four pairs of limbs and one or more pairs of feeding appendages	shrimp, crabs, woodlice and barnacles
	Myriapods	land-living animals with many legs on a long segmented body, one pair of antennae	millipedes, centipedes
	Arachnids	land-living, eight-legged animals, without antennae	scorpions, spiders, ticks and mites
	Insects	land-living six-legged animals, one pair of antennae and often two pairs of wings; body divided into three parts – the head, thorax and abdomen	wasps, butterflies, cockroaches, dragonflies, beetles, ants, flies
Vertebrates (animals with backbones)	Fish	water-living, cold-blooded animals, breathing through gills; generally muscular bodies, covered in scales, with fins for swimming; skeleton can be made of bone or cartilage; most reproduce by laying eggs in water	sharks, dogfish (cartilage skeletons) – salmon, cod, seahorses, eels, trout, (bony skeletons)
	Amphibians	cold-blooded animals with two-stage life cycle, larvae live in water and have gills, adults live on land and have lungs but swim well; moist skin without scales, eggs are laid in water	frogs, newts
	Reptiles	mostly land-living cold-blooded animals breathing through lungs; dry, waterproof skin covered in scales; most are four-legged though some (the snakes) have none; eggs, protected by soft shells, are laid on land.	crocodiles, lizards, tortoises, snakes
	Birds	warm-blooded, land-living animals breathing through lungs; most have wings and can fly; skin is covered in feathers, a characteristic only birds have; all have beaks for feeding; eggs, protected by hard shells, are laid in nests	sparrow, ostriches, eagles, parrots
	Mammals	warm-blooded animals, breathing through lungs, found in a variety of habitats on land and in water; some (bats) can fly; all have at least some hair; young generally develop inside the mother and are born live and fed on milk produced by the mother	egg-laying examples, such as the duck-billed platypus; pouched examples (the marsupials), such as kangaroos and koalas, which give birth to a young that develope in a pouch on the mother; placental examples, such as cats, elephants, bears and humans, which give birth to well-developed young

Glossary

alveolus (plural alveoli) thin-walled, microscopic air sac in the lung where oxygen diffuses from the lung into the blood and carbon dioxide diffuses out from the blood into the lung

amino acids naturally occuring chemicals used by cells to make proteins

antibody a defensive protein produced by white blood cells in response to the presence of foreign organisms (antigens) such as viruses or bacteria. Each antibody reacts to one type of antigen and combines with it to render it harmless or to destroy it.

antigen any molecule that the immune system recognizes as a foreign substance triggering the production of antibodies; typical antigens are the proteins on the surface of bacteria and viruses

asexual reproduction any of a number of ways of reproducing by which offspring arise from a single parent and are genetically identical to that parent

axon an extension from the cell body of a neurone, specialized for the transmission of nerve impulses

bacterium (plural bacteria) microscopic single-celled organism that does not have a nucleus

Bowman's capsule cup-shaped part of a nephron that receives water and dissolved substances filtered from blood in the kidney

brain stem region where the top of the spinal cord merges with the bottom of the brain. Activities such as heart rate, breathing and blood pressure are regulated here

bronchioles a fine tube in the lungs of reptiles, birds and mammals

carbohydrate chemical compound composed of carbon, hydrogen and oxygen used by the body as a source of energy. Glucose is the simplest carbohydrate.

cerebellum part of the brain where reflex centres are found; responsible for posture and limb movements

cerebrum part of the brain responsible for most information processing in mammals

chromosone a DNA molecule coiled around protein molecules called listones. Chromosones are present in the nuclei of eukaryote cells. During nuclear division, they become visible as rod-like structures.

cilia (singular **cilium**) thin, hair-like structures that project in large numbers from some cells

cytoplasm all of the parts of a cell between the nucleus and the cell membrane

dendrite a fine extension of a nerve cell that receives impulses from other nerve cells

embryo early developmental stage of a plant or animal formed by cell division after fertilization of an egg

endocrine gland gland that produces hormones for release into the bloodstream

endoskeleton an internal supporting skeleton, made of cartilage or bone

enzymes biological catalysts that greatly speed up the reactions that take place in cells; all enzymes are proteins

epithelial (epithelium) type of tissue made up of closely packed cells that forms an outer surface or lines a cavity or tube

eukaryotes cells that contain a nucleus and other organelles; all cells with the exception of bacteria are eukaryote cells

excretion the removal of waste products from cells

exoskeleton a hard, rigid covering on the outside of the body in some animals, such as insects

extensor a muscle that straightens a limb

fertilization the fusing together of two sex cells, or gametes

flexor a muscle that bends a limb

gamete a sex cell such as a sperm or an egg

gills organs used for respiration by fish and other aquatic animals

glomerulus cluster of blood capillaries in the kidney where water and dissolved substances are filtered from the blood

glucose the simplest carbohydrate, made by plants during photosynthesis and used by all cells as a source of energy in respiration

Golgi body a structure inside a cell responsible for packaging proteins and other substances manufactered inside the cell ready for export

homeostasis the maintenance of the internal environment of an organism at ideal levels for cell activities to be carried out

hormone chemical produced by the endochrine glands that is concerned with the regulation of body functions such as blood sugar levels

hydrostatic skeleton skeleton in which the muscles work against an internal body fluid

immune not susceptible to infection

invertebrates animals without backbones

lactic acid the waste product of one form of anaerobic respiration

lipid a greasy or oily substance; fats are lipids

marrow soft fatty substance found in cavities inside bones

mast cell a cell that produces histamine as part of the immune system's response to infection

membrane layer of protein and fat molecules that encloses a cell

metabolism the sum total of all the chemical reactions in a cell

minerals simple chemicals required by living organisms to maintain health

mitochondria (singular **mitochondrion**) the structure within the cell where aerobic respiration takes place; they produce a cell's energy

motor neurone see **neurone**

mucus slimy substance that protects and lubricates mucous membranes

myelin material made of fats and proteins that insulates nerve cells

nephron one of the tubules in the kidney where urine is formed

neurone (**motor**, **sensory**) a nerve cell responsible for transmitting impulses through the body

nucleus (**plural nuclei**) large organelle in the centre of a cell where its genetic material is held

nutrients the chemicals needed by a living organism in order for it to live, grow and maintain health

oesophagus muscular tube down which food travels from the mouth to the stomach

offspring the young of an animal

organelles structures in cells, such as mitochondria and Golgi bodies, that are responsible for carrying out various tasks in the cell

osmosis the movement of water from a weak solution through a partially permeable membrane to a stronger solution

ovary the organ in female animals from which eggs are produced

oviduct tube down which eggs travel from the ovary to the uterus

phagocyte type of white blood cell that engulfs and consumes other cells

placenta organ found in pregnant female mammals that attaches to the inside of the uterus and allows the exchange of nutrients, oxygen and waste products between the bloodstreams of mother and young

plasma the liquid part of blood

prokaryotes cells that do not have their genetic material in a nucleus; all bacteria are prokaryotes

protein one of a group of complex organic molecules that perform a variety of essential tasks in cells, including providing structure and acting as catalysts (enzymes) in chemical reactions

protisans a diverse grouping of microscopic single-celled organisms

receptor part of a cell that receives information from elsewhere, for instance from a nerve cell or by receiving a hormone molecule

respiration process by which all organisms obtain energy from food, by breaking down sugars into simpler substances. Anaerobic respiration can take place without oxygen. Aerobic respiration is a much more efficient process that requires oxygen to work.

sensory neurone see **neurone**

sexual reproduction reproduction involving the joining together of sex cells, such as eggs and sperm

sperm male sex cells

synapse junction between nerve cells

tendon connective tissue joining muscle to bone

testes the organ in male animals in which the sperm are produced

trachea tube that conducts air down into the lungs

tubule a small fine tube found in the kidneys of animals

umbilical cord connection between the placenta and the growing embryo

uterus the organ in female mammals in which the embryo develops

vagina part of the reproductive system in female mammals that receives sperm from the male

vertebrates animals with backbones

virus a non-living agent composed of DNA or RNA in a protein coat that is capable of infecting a cell and taking over its metabolic machinery to make copies of itself

vitamin one of a number of substances that organisms require in small amounts in their diets for metabolism

Further reading and websites

Books

Coordinated Science: Higher Biology, Richard Fosbery, Jean McLean, Heinemann Library, 1996

Life, David Burnie, Dorling Kindersley Eyewitness Guides, 1998

Life Processes: Cells and Systems and *Classification*, Holly Wallace, Heinemann Library, 2001

The Living Planet, David Attenborough, BBC Consumer Publishing (Books), 1994

The Trials of Life, David Attenborough, Collins, 1992

Websites

Animals in Danger (http://www.unep-wcmc.org/)
Concentrates on endangered species and the work of the World Conservation Monitoring Centre

Online Exhibition (http://www.nhm.ac.uk/)
Shows the collections and exhibitions of the Natural History Museum, London

Voyage Through the Life Sciences
(http://www.life.uiuc.edu/plantbio/102/links.html)
A multitude of links for internet travel in the life sciences

Web of Life (http://www.weboflife.co.uk/weboflife/index.html)
An exhibition showing the variety and interaction between the different forms of life on Earth

Zoology on the Internet (http://www.biosis.org.uk/free_resources/resource_guide.html)
Animals, animals and more animals, with many links to other websites

Index